J. M. Loughridge

2.12.2000

Edinburgh
German Church Bazaar
(free)

how to survive abroad

spike hughes

how to survive abroad

Drawings by Mel Calman

methuen

First published in 1971
by Methuen and Co Ltd
11 New Fetter Lane, London EC4
Text © 1971 by Spike Hughes
Drawings © 1971 by Mel Calman
Filmset by Layton-Sun Ltd
6-10 Kirby Street, London EC1
Printed in Great Britain
by Butler & Tanner Ltd
Frome and London

SBN 416 66120 3

to my sister

angela baignères

and to

charmian

who also tells me the answers,
and does the packing

contents

"Away! Take heed; I will abroad" – George Herbert

To survive, my dictionary tells me, is "to continue to exist in spite of children, contemporaries, etc.", and – as if children and contemporaries were something quite different – "all perils". The term "all perils" sounds comprehensive enough, but I doubt if the perils the lexicographer had in mind included any of those which confront the English traveller abroad.

The English can claim to be easily the world's most travelled race. They not only survived furthest-flung Abroad; they owned most of it. For centuries their survival was based on the simple practice of maintaining, wherever they went, what is so smugly known as the English Way of Life (and what a way *that* has been leading us recently).

In their imposition of their Way of Life on others who might have preferred – given a chance – their own way of living, the English did the most reprehensible things. The worst of these was the criminally careless loss of a possession which produced the greatest wine and some of the best food in the world. This dominion contained such centres of souse-and-guzzle as Bayonne and Bordeaux, Cognac, Armagnac and Périgueux, Rouen and Brittany.

Bordeaux was English for three hundred years, until one of our fool monarchs let the French have it back, as though it were America or somewhere.

It was only a matter of time, however, before the English, led by the Irish, returned quietly to the Bordelais and established wine businesses – about forty of them – with labels bearing names like Lynch and Talbot, Hennessy and Kirwan, Brown, Palmer and Château Smith-Haut Laffitte.

Elsewhere in Europe, re-infiltration was equally thorough. If a couple of Englishmen met in any French or Italian town with a good winter climate, within a couple of months the place would have an English tennis club, church, golf links, library (with tea-room attached), newspaper and doctor.

Today, the clubs and libraries and medical practices, the *Riviera Post* and the *Mentone and Monte Carlo News* have disappeared or been taken over by the natives, but many of the English churches – a little surprisingly – still function.

The English who cultivated these foreign fields, whose unique skill in surviving abroad in comfort, splendour and complete ignorance of any language but their own, flourished from the beginning of the nineteenth century until the 1920s. Then the race died out, its fame commemorated by a thousand hotels all over Europe called the Bristol, the Brighton, the Hotel d'Osborne, the Albergo Dover, and the memorable Hôtel de Bade et O'Connor, a spacious, four-posted, stately-home-from-stately-home in Nice.

HOW TO SURVIVE BEING CALLED ENGLISH

I must apologize to my fellow-Celts for the constant use in this manual of the term "English", but the Irish, Welsh and Scots, if they wish to survive abroad, must learn to accept with good grace the solecism of being regarded by all foreigners as English. Except in official or political contexts "British" is used as a noun habitually and unselfconsciously only by the Americans. This usage dates back to the War of Independence, when they wanted a term to cover the English Army, their German Sovereign and his 22,000 Hessian mercenaries. In general, however, foreigners are not aware of any difference between the four races inhabiting the British

Isles. Nevertheless, it is sometimes worth proclaiming and exploiting your Celtic origin when confronted by natives who are being tiresomely anglophobic.

In France they are constantly aware of the Auld Alliance; it influences their choice of whisky, and inspires a chain of their supermarkets to use the brand name "Kilt" for all its products, from sardines and envelopes, to wine and ambidextrous potato peelers.

In Germany and Russia, if they learn you are Irish, they will express more intensely than ever their admiration of Shaw and Wilde; and in most countries anywhere, the Welsh will be credited with having cradled the famous Prince of Wales who was Edward VIII for a time.

But for the most part we are all indiscriminately regarded as English. Incorrigibly so; for what hope have we when the standard French translation of "Rule, Britannia!" is still "Gouverne, Angleterre!"?

BUREAUCRATS' PROGRESS

The idea that there has been progress in all aspects of foreign travel since the 1914-18 war is one of the illusions of our age. Jets and motorways may be all very wonderful, but without benefit of either it was still possible in 1913 to travel to France and Italy, for instance, without a passport or papers of any kind, and with sovereigns and half-sovereigns, pennies and half-pennies in your pocket that were accepted as legal tender over the counter of half the shops in Europe.

The only use of a passport was to identify yourself when you collected your *poste restante* letters (though a visiting card would do), and to enable you to visit museums and picture galleries when they were closed to the public. Unfortunately, the first war to end war, which ended, of course, in a peace to end peace, put an end to all this too.

The fact that we can survive, or even try to survive, abroad in the conditions we now have to endure, demonstrates once and for all that though we may be decadent, insignificant in world affairs and unable to spend our money how and where we like, we have lost none of our traditional gift of improvisation and unflinching courage in the face of disaster.

The english complaint

Let it be said at once, that to survive abroad, it is not enough merely to improvise and be courageous. Improvisation and courage will not, for instance, cure the diarrhoea that afflicts all but the most experienced and knowledgeable English traveller in Europe.

This distressing complaint, which has ruined more holidays than rain and inconvenienced more honeymooners than virginity, is not, as so many sufferers believe, the fault of the foreign food they are given when abroad. In fact, it occurs to package-tourists who eat nothing but eggs on chips and H P Sauce.

THEORY

In my experience, it's really all to do with nerves, with nothing more nor less than what in childhood always ended in tears: becoming over-excited.

It may seem ridiculous to suggest that the grown-up English should ever get over-excited by such a simple, centuries-old national recreation as going abroad, but it is surprising what effect a mild tranquillizer and a trouble-free outward journey can have on the rest of one's holiday.

See Venice
and run

W.C.

THERAPY

If you are still unlucky, and do catch a bug, or forgot to remember that figs, which make syrup of figs, are not the best fruit to gorge yourself on, there are nowadays plenty of remedies.

The best, Guanamycin, unfortunately isn't available on the National Health – at least, not until you are actually suffering. Which isn't much help if you are in St Tropez or Capri at the onset of the trouble. But if you will pay for it, a thoughtful G.P. will prescribe a bottle to take with you in case you need it. When you do need it, mix it with water and take it according to instructions. The reason you don't take it already mixed is that once diluted it is effective for only a week. It also weighs more than unmixed.

PROPHYLAXIS

Nature has its own cures. Rice is said to be one. But prevention being better than cure we have not found anything to compare with the prophylactic property of the mere possession of our bottles of neat Guanamycin. This is pure auto-suggestion, of course, but it works.

Getting there

There was a time when Abroad was said to begin at Calais, because that was the nearest point to England that foreigners were encountered in the mass. By this reckoning Abroad today begins at Piccadilly Circus. If we accept that once you are on your journey you are abroad, the dangers that have to be survived differ not only from one means of transport to another, but from traveller to traveller. Experiences on the way there and on the way back can be highly individual, and therefore difficult to anticipate and provide for in a book like this.

What happens while we're actually there, on the other hand, seems to be common to all – whatever country we go to, and wherever we finish up, whether in villas, pensions, flats, caravans, yachts, tents, or roughing it at the Negresco.

My own preference has always been for travel by hard-surface transport – that is, by rail or road – which involves one sooner with the natives than going by air or all the way by sea. But however often one travels, and by whatever means, each occasion proves more forcibly than the last the folly of relying on precedent. Despite olde-time memories and long-established precedents of French porters at the Gare St Lazare in Paris, trampling each other underfoot to get your custom, we recently arrived there on a Sunday and the only porter to be seen was one we eventually found propping up the zinc bar of one of the station buffets.

TRAIN DE DEMI-LUXE

We crossed Paris and continued our journey from the Gare de Lyon, by the Blue Train – an elegant, comfortable and romantic train if ever there was one. We dined well, slept well, and in the morning pulled up the blind of the *wagon-lit* to see, in the glowing red sunlight of a Provence morning, mile after mile of *tableaux vivants* by Cézanne.

We went along to the restaurant car. Breakfast, we knew according to precedent, would be delicious. The Blue Train was famous for its breakfast. Alas, for precedent: the restaurant of the Blue Train served Nescafé. The French regard Nescafé as *très chic*.

In spite of this shocking experience which, if it is a permanent development, one can only try to shrug off philosophically with the thought that breakfast doesn't last for ever, there is a great leisurely olde-worlde attraction in travelling under the flag of the International Company of the Waggon-Beds and of the Large European Expresses. You can still get into a sleeper at Calais, change into your slippers, and make the train a comfortable home for as far as the coach will take you – Istanbul even, some people say.

TOO COMPRIS

We don't do this sort of thing every time, of course, only as an occasional change. Last time we set out to do it, the French railways went on strike and we had to fly instead. Owing to an administrative slip-up on my part, we found ourselves going First Class by mistake in a Caravelle to Nice.

And what, you may ask, is there to survive in that –

its the only way to fly

apart from falling through the floor of the aircraft, being hi-jacked, or bursting a tyre on landing (which has happened to me before now)?

I'll tell you. We took off at 10.20 a.m. At 10.40 luncheon was served – a real four-course hot-midday-dinner they called *déjeuner*. There was champagne, burgundy, brandy, a searing hot *tournedos Rossini* that burnt your tongue. Air France was determined to treat us well for the fare we paid, and we were equally determined to eat and drink as much as possible to justify the difference between the First Class and Tourist fares – about £24 each, I think it was.

Unfortunately, we reached Nice before we could drink anywhere near twenty-four pounds' worth of champagne, so the battle was lost. We had another shot on the return journey, but again we failed to survive the challenge.

In the end we prefer to travel by car; for while it's pleasant to watch the scenery from the train and have no responsibility for driving it, at least going by road you don't have to miss the best bits because you're asleep – that is, unless you have had too big a lunch.

MEALS ON WHEELS

One way of getting the best of both worlds is to use the car-sleeper which, of course, presents another set of survival problems. The most formidable of these is to get dinner on the train in a civilized manner. The fact that you have booked dinner and have a ticket to prove it, means absolutely nothing. You must anticipate the *premier service* (you'll starve to death waiting for the *deuxième*) by going along to the dining car, waiting until the door is opened and then making a dash for it.

If – as we once did – you wait obediently until the steward comes along the corridor, ringing his bell, you can find yourself and your nearest and dearest sitting at separate tables out of sight and ear-shot of each other. The hope of getting an aperitif in the dining car before you are half way through dinner is usually pretty forlorn. It is best to have a whacking great slug on the station before you leave, or carry a hip flask and take nips out of it while you wait for the doors to open.

The Waggon-Beds Company's habit of stocking only half-bottles of wine I find a particularly miserable one. Ordering two halves is somehow more ostentatious, and looks more intemperate, than ordering one whole bottle. One thing is absolutely essential, however, if you are likely to want two half-bottles order them both as soon as the steward takes orders. If you don't, the chances of ever getting the other half are very slim. Stewards become blind and deaf to all waving and whistling to attract their attention once dinner is underway. On the Boulogne-Milan run, incidentally, you can count on the Château Batailley.

The advantages of the car-sleeper route on the outward journey far outweigh those – if any – of the inward journey. Going out, you start your holiday feeling rested after a good night's sleep (no better sleeping draught than a couple of large brandies with your coffee).

Coming back, from all accounts (we have never tried it ourselves), the food is poor, the service slapdash, and the whole attitude of the stewards is that anything will do for the English. Why there should be so much difference between the two journeys nobody has yet been able to explain, but it seems to be a common feature of the second stages of there-and-back car-sleeper travel. For ourselves, we prefer that withdrawal from abroad should be a gradual, gentle process, with pleasant side-effects, punctuated by overnight stops after a short, unhurried day's driving, and as far as possible at places we have not been to before.

Staying the night

The most frequently recurrent problem is where to stay the night. Some people try to solve it by driving like hell until seven o'clock and then looking for a hotel.

This, one soon learns, is a frustrating, hit-or-miss process; hotels on any conveniently main road have been filled by native motorists long before you get there, and the search for other accommodation can be a long one.

Other people, less reckless, drive like hell until five o'clock and are usually certain of finding what they want – that is, if they have previously decided where they want to be about five o'clock.

ENJOYING THE NIGHT

The most cautious, and most successful, method is to decide where to aim for without having to drive like hell to get there. Experience has taught us to telephone the Hotel at B immediately on arrival at the Hotel at A. Leaving it until next morning can sometimes be too late, and you find yourself not only failing to find another hotel at B, but often having to go to another town altogether.

There are few things more comforting and more conducive to enjoying a good dinner tonight than knowing where you are going to enjoy a good dinner tomorrow.

YOUR NAME, PLEASE?

Giving your name on the telephone is a bit tricky. If you are doing your own telephoning anywhere in Europe it is essential to know the alphabet. Better still, however, is to get somebody else to make the call for you. They won't attempt to pronounce the unpronounceable, but will spell it out automatically.

If by some mischance you are forced to struggle with the telephone on your own, and your name is Loughborough, Etheridge, Bretherton, Lightfoot or Woodward and you don't know the alphabet, the safest thing to do is to invent a good international code-name for yourself – like Mac, Tommy, Luna, Oxo or Bromo.

LOOK BEFORE YOU SLEEP

The first thing to do when you eventually reach your hotel and have identified yourself, is to have a look at the room they offer you. See that the bedside lights work, that there's a plug for your razor, that the beds are clean and comfortable, that there are two glasses by the basin.

Next time I ask for a room with a bath, I'll make sure there's also a bed in it

(The razor plug is important, though ever since a visit to Spain I have personally always travelled with a battery-driven razor. In one Spanish hotel the only light of any kind was on the ceiling, and to shave I had to stand on the bed, dismantle a glass bowl shade, and having connected my razor with the bulb socket, continue to stand on the bed while I shaved; the lead of the razor was too short for me to do anything else. This sort of obstacle race also stresses the advantage of the battery-driven toothbrush.)

If you don't like the room, ask to see another. This demand will surprise them no end, for the English notoriously take what they're given and do not complain. But here you are, the English, asking to see the room before you take it – as though you were a native, looking at what he's expected to pay for.

The hotel's initial surprise will now turn to respect, and if they have another unoccupied room they will show it you.

OH, YES – AND PILLOWS

Whichever room you end up in, if you are in France you will now have to ask for pillows and a second bath towel. The pillows are never on the beds, but usually tucked away in the wardrobe by a management who shares the hope of every one of its kind all over France: that you will sleep with the hard sausage-shaped bolster which is covered by the bottom sheet, and so save them the expense of laundering pillow cases.

TOWELS, SOAP

The single bath towel invariably found in the bathrooms of double rooms is also to save laundry. Send

I know there's no hot water, no telephone, no lift, no room service, no towel — but you can't have everything :

for the second towel. One must not encourage the French any further in their more irritatingly peculiar penny-pinching habits.

If there is any soap in your hotel it will be a miracle; but then you knew that when you packed soap in your luggage before you left home. However, this situation is improving, at any rate in France.

You will find soap in your room in all the comfortable hotels on the chain known nauseatingly as "The Little Nests of France" – *Les Petits Nids de France*. Elsewhere, where they proudly proclaim their premises have been *modernisé* (which means that bathrooms and lavatories have been installed with curtains instead of doors), you not only find soap donated by Worth, but toothpaste, and a free copy of *Le Figaro* and the local daily with breakfast.

Thirst things first

Having long ago failed to find a palatably dry aperitif in Europe (except in Spain and then with difficulty), I always make a point of carrying gin and whisky with me on my travels, and taking them into the hotel, what's more.

A cad's trick, of course. But it's well worth feeling caddish, especially at the start of your journey when you still have your duty-free bottles with you.

In France, when you are ready for your drink, go strike upon the bell and ask them to send up "un Schweppes" and "un quart [which is a quarter not a quart] de Perrier", or a large bottle of whatever mineral water you will inevitably want to drink in the night.

Your request for these items will not arouse suspicion. The French drink Schweppes (don't ask for "tonic"; the word means nothing to them) as a drink on its own, sitting in cafés for hours with a single glass of it in front of them. Perrier and other mineral waters are also respectable soft drinks, but not so smart as "le Schweppes".

With the gradual spread of Schweppes' tonic water all over Europe, this method ensures that your evening gin is drunk in the form to which you are accustomed. And if by an awful chance some Italian hotel has no Schweppes, you can always order an *americano* (Campari and red vermouth) and add your gin to it to make what the French call *le long drink* into a Negroni.

NOT ONLY THAT, BUT IT'S CHEAPER

Naturally, unless you have smuggled in more than you're allowed, duty-free bottles don't last forever. But many English travellers don't seem to realize that in France and Italy (and elsewhere, for all I know) gin and whisky can be bought for less – thanks to one Budget after another – than ever it is in England, and is indistinguishable from what you get at home, except that gin is eighty per cent proof instead of seventy per cent. Which means that you can use slightly less, or getting stinking quicker, whichever is the more likely.

More surprising, is the reasonable price of Scotch. Avoid the popular brands like the plague. The *chic* enjoyed by Johnnie Walker, for instance, benefits only the wholesaler and retailer. On the shelves of small shops all over Europe you will find good whisky from small distilleries you have probably never heard of. Their names are not popular, but their prices are.

Is this being horribly insular, this liking for gin and whisky? Probably. But in any case, to drink whisky abroad nowadays is almost to drink the *vin de pays*: when you drink whisky in Rome, you literally do as the Romans do.

LE LONG DRINK: KIDS' STUFF

As a disinterested observer, I have to remark on the quite astonishing variety of non-alcoholic syrups and fizzes that have been invented, and continue to be invented, in the more famous drinking countries. The English traveller with children can choose from a vast repertoire of sweet soft drinks – the best of which, I remember from my brief teetotal childhood, were the pomegranate syrup called Grenadine, and the rich Italian orange-concentrate, *aranciata*, dispensed from great glass tanks. To see what children are offered nowadays, you have only to look on the packed shelves of any foreign café.

And, of course, when all other temptations fail, there is always Coca-Cola – an inspired example of the universally understood and pronounceable name, like gas, kodak or Piccadilly.

Finally, for the teenager who likes to learn from his own kind abroad, as well as teach them something, there is the very popular French drink called "Wel-Scotch". This is a kind of porter and is considered *très snob* by the young, who drink it diluted with tonic water.

LE LONG DRINK:
KIDS' PARENTS' STUFF

The adult English traveller with a thirst, accompanied by children or not, can also choose from a wide repertoire of sweet, but alcoholic drinks, some of them based on wine, some on spirits, some of them intended as liqueurs, some as aperitifs, some as long drinks, and some as simple antibiotic mouthwash.

Unlike his children, who are faced with a *richesse* which doesn't for a moment embarrass, let alone deter them from trying everything once, the adult traveller has to be less adventurous. He can well be what the Irish call "parlattic" before he finds a drink he can tolerate if *he* starts methodically trying everything once.

The long drink presents the biggest problem, unless you stick to draught beer (*pression* in France).

In Germany and Austria, the request for *ein gespritzter* will produce the refreshing equivalent of Byron's hock and seltzer. The alkali of the soda water seems to cancel out the high acidity of the wine, and so makes an unpromising drink really quite tolerable. It affords a welcome change in the summer from all that beer.

You must put out of your head at once any idea that instead of drinking either, you can sit in a *Weinstube*, or wine-snug, and enjoy a good bottle of hock or moselle. You won't find that easily in Germany or Austria, not even in restaurants; and when you do, it usually costs more than it does in England. But that's international economic hanky-panky all over.

Once across the channel, red Martini or Cinzano (long

you know you
are supposed to
drink aperitifs
before meals —
not instead of...

gallicized as *san-zanno*) is mixed with every conceivable syrup and cordial, and when poured out liberally into a tall glass with a lump of ice, a slice of lemon, and filled up with soda, will make you one of the best long drinks in the world.

More obvious and, for many people, more adventurous, long drinks are the aniseed concoctions ranging from ouzo in Greece to the numberless variations on this very limited theme in Italy, France and Spain.

For the Pernod addict I would recommend the coast above Alicante, where we were once astonished, twice pie-eyed, in a roadside hotel bar where the stuff was poured out, half-a-pint at a time, in tall Tom Collins tumblers. The cost, like the amount of water you could add, was negligible.

Back in France Pernod and the various *pastis* are not sloshed around quite so recklessly as in that Spanish bar. Which is as well, for a couple of *pastis* drunk in the Mediterranean sun are enough, if one's palate for anything else is not to be anaesthetized for two or three hours.

LE SHORT DRINK

The true aperitif, as distinct from the drink you have before a meal because you happen to be thirsty, is a perpetual problem abroad. The best-known French brands can be tried out in England. Lillet, Byrrh, Saint-Raphaël, Dubonnet, Cap Corse, and various brands of Chambéry, are found in most good pubs and off-licenses up and down the country.

Unfortunately, the only one that is difficult to find in France is also, for many people, the best: vermouth from Chambéry. It is not just that so many French cafés don't stock it; most of them have never even heard of it.

This is a result of that fierce regionalism which is still as firmly established in France, Spain and Italy as it was in the Middle Ages. Regionalism of this kind can be most infectious, and I was indignantly surprised on my first visit to Devonshire to discover that the price of Plymouth Gin was the same there as in John o'Groats, Southend or Derrygonnelly.

ANDALUSIA SHERRY TYPE

Catalonia, they will tell you, isn't Spain; it certainly isn't Andalusia either.

My brother-in-law Tony, who had served part of his apprenticeship in the wine trade at Jerez, counselled us when in Spain to order Tio Pepe by the half-bottle in cafés and bars; it was much cheaper. The practice in Andalusia was no doubt general and accepted; but on the Costa Brava (this was in pre-package-tour days), even the name "Tio Pepe" was regarded as something foreign, probably English, specially imported for foreigners, like Bass and Guinness. On our asking for a half-bottle of Tio Pepe, a whole bottle was opened, and half of it poured into an empty bottle. From this now half-full (or half-empty) second bottle, the sherry was transferred, a glass at a time, into yet another empty bottle. The number of glassfuls was reckoned up and we were charged for our half bottle at the rate per glass. By the time this process had been completed and the Tio Pepe had been put before us, the sherry was nice and warm, and owing to wastage, spillage, sloppage, and evaporation, was noticeably less than half a bottle, and cost us roughly what the same amount would have cost in an English pub.

PRELUDIO

In Italy, where the entire population seems to suffer from its *fegato* (which is not Italian for a bassoon, but for the liver), the *aperitivo* becomes a matter of pharmacy.

In his perpetual and apparently hopeless attempt to stimulate what, at first sight, hardly seems to be a very reluctant appetite, the modern Italian adopts drastic methods based on the arts of the mediaeval herbalists, making use – to judge by the taste – of the peculiar philhepatic properties of ragwort, jack-in-the-hedge, curare and potato peel. At any rate, a nation that has to resort in desperation to drinks made of artichoke, rhubarb, quinine and Friar's balsam before it can face its feed, must now really have tried everything once.

Always excepting straight red vermouth, the best true aperitif in Italy is the *americano* – Campari, red vermouth and a touch of soda water. The addition of gin turns it into a Negroni and at once deprives the *americano* of most of its character.

If you are ever in Milan, where Campari is made, there is a Campari Bar at the corner of the Galleria and the Piazza del Duomo. It is small, noisy, uncomfortable, and designed for those who are content to stand at the bar and drink Campari straight from the fountain head.

If you have never tasted an *americano*, this is the place to start.

FINALE

The question of the *digestivo*, the end-of-the-meal drink, in Italy is the biggest headache of all. The fact that they refer to it as a *digestivo* instead of a *liquore* is an ominous declaration of Italian priorities. It is a drink not to enjoy, but to do you good.

The *digestivo* can be made of almost anything, and usually is – walnuts, aloe, camomile, Peruvian bark, aniseed, grape skins, cherry stones, rhubarb, apricots, roots, leaves, honey, flower stalks. Only the witches in *Macbeth* ever cooked up anything with more startling ingredients.

After a meal, to my taste, the only thing to drink in Italy is *grappa*, distilled, like *marc*, from the skins, pips and stalks of grapes. Before dinner you can knock it back like vodka.

WATERS OF LIFE

In France the question of the drink for *après-nosh* is not so complicated, even allowing for the fact that good cognac hardly exists there any more. It is too much to expect the class of brandy you drink in your own home (if you have the sense to belong to the Wine Society), but you do expect the French to be able to produce something better than the dark brown, caramel-tainted, abrasive and indigestible spirit that passes for cognac nowadays – and with such once-honourable names on the labels, too. The only thing to do is to drink Armagnac instead. Up to now they haven't mucked about with it and it is what the wine-jargonauts would call "honest". And after Armagnac there is Marc de Bourgogne which, when you're lucky, can be as smooth as silk.

The *eaux-de-vie* can be good, too, but it is important to be clear about the differences between them. Something called simply *eau-de-vie*, or *eau-de-vie-de*-somewhere-or-other will be brandy or distilled wine of some potency and fire, but of no distinct flavour.

An *eau-de-vie* which states that it is *de framboise, de poires, de myrtilles, de mirabelles, de quetsch, de prunes, de fruits, de cidres*, means that it is distilled from, and tastes of, what the label says. All brands of Calvados are *eaux-de-vie-de-cidres*, but unfortunately not all *eaux-de-vie-de-cidres* are Calvados.

The Swiss produce an excellent *eau-de-vie* made from William pears and called Williamine. But it tends to be a bit costly, for as John Evelyn noted around 1646, the Swiss have "a great honestie and fidelity, tho' exacting enough for what they part with."

Tipping

DRINKS

The only rule to remember about tipping abroad is to remember to tip.

If it is a café with a cash register that produces a ticket which is brought to you with your drink, it will state on it whether service is, or is not, included in the total shown.

In many parts of abroad this information is also shown in English – a practice which succeeds in antagonising both the English and all the other foreigners who use that particular café. The English are insulted by the presumption that they don't understand any other language; the others are insulted by the implication that the only foreign customers are English. And both sides are insulted when they realize that the whole thing is done for the benefit of the Americans, who are notoriously bad tippers anyway, and are likely to take no notice of anything except the figures in the total.

If the ticket states that service is included, you still leave a few coins – the smaller bits of change that comes back to you. If it is not included, then your long and arduous experience of English decimal currency will make it easy for you to work out twelve or fifteen per cent of the total and leave that.

Where, as often happens, there is no ticket at all, and you ask how much you owe, you must also ask whether service is included.

Introducing a carefully-produced interrogatory note into the voice you ask in France "Service compris?", in Italy "Servizio compreso?"

In Spain the phrase is "¿Servicio includo?", though whether you adopt a two-tone voice for the two question marks, or ask the question twice, standing on your head the second time, has never been made quite clear. In Sweden you say "Inklusiv service?" and in Denmark "Er det met drikke-penge?".

Nine times out of ten the answer to these questions will be "No". You then do your sums as before. If the answer is "Yes", you leave the usual chicken-feed.

As for change to do all this with, few waiters are fool-hardy enough not to provide you with this. Those who are, and leave behind a single large-denomination coin which is far more than you should tip them, must be sent away for change – *monnaie* in French, *Kleingeld* in German, *moneta* in Italian, *moneda* in Spanish.

On no account, however, go away without tipping. There is no Catering Wages Act abroad.

RAILWAY PORTERS

If you can ever find a porter when you want one, railway stations abroad display the official tariff for his services – if you can ever find it when you want it.

In Italy it is usually on show in the booking hall, and the rates vary according to where you are. They are highest in Rome, lowest in Sicily. The tariff is so much for each piece of luggage. You pay that and add a little something for himself, your good man.

I can't remember where the tariff is shown in France, but if it's the only word you say to any porter in any country, "tariff" (pronounced with a Yorkshire "a" and spoken in a stern and authoritative tone of voice) will make him think you are aware of any tricks he might otherwise get up to. He may sometimes take a chance, and reasoning (quite rightly) that you don't know the tariff anyway, ask for more than the official rate. But in most cases he won't gamble on it.

PATRONAGE OF THE ARTS

Naples is the place that leads you into a lot of unexpected tipping, for the Neapolitan restaurant involves you with the Neapolitan musician. He wanders from one place to another, sings two verses of "Santa Lucia" at you at the top of his voice (just because Caruso was born in Naples isn't really enough), and then takes the hat round.

Native diners do not seem to resent this, and donate charitable chicken-feed without hesitation. You, of course, will do the same, though for myself I do it with a reluctance it is a superhuman task to conceal. The wandering minstrel who infests the restaurants of Europe is no doubt a romantic figure, but for the musical there is no more excruciating torture on earth than the unwanted, inescapable music, both live and recorded, which our philistine civilization scatters like the rest of its litter.

We hear a lot of international talk about polluting the air. It is time somebody said something international about polluting the ear.

Privy counsel

Foreign cafés, hotels and restaurants inevitably involve the traveller in that unending struggle with the really astonishing international reluctance to call a water-closet a W.C., even though the letters are in common use in the Michelin Guides and on the doors of the lavatories themselves.

The trouble is that the euphemisms are so often ambiguous. In English "lavatory" now has only one meaning. But knowing from childhood that the French "cabinet" was a recognised euphemism for the W.C., like "gabinetto" in Italian, it was disconcerting to find once at Aix-en-Provence that the room we had booked "avec bain et cabinet privé" was literally a bathroom, and a "cabinet de toilette" which proved to be a curtained-off alcove with a basin and bidet. So much for the face value of another euphemism: "May I go to the bathroom?"

Once you are downstairs in France, in the restaurant or wherever, the genteel English euphemism "toilet" can be translated back into the language where it belongs. Ask for "la toilette" and you will be shown what you need.

Sometimes, if you are a man, you may be surprised to find an elderly woman attendant in the Gents'. She is directly descended from the *tricoteuses* of the French Revolution. Today she knits waiting, not for aristocratic heads to drop into a basket, but for your plebian coins to drop into the saucer lying prominently on a table beside her.

Tip her half of the highest single coin she leaves as a nest-egg on the saucer.

LOOPHEMISMS

What might be a euphemism in one language is very often used literally in another. The word "lavabo" on a French door has raised the hopes of thousands of English travellers by its similarity to "lavatory", and dashed them by offering a place to wash in, fitted with a basin, a cold tap, no soap, and a very grubby, worn towel (if any).

All that "lavabo" means is that the French know the Latin for "I will wash", and you don't.

The Spanish "el retrete" means water-closet, and with its suggestion of peace and quiet comes near to the old English word (still current in the U.S.A.) "privy".

The same principle is encountered in the sign seen in Germany and Austria which announces "Abort". In case you are puzzled or alarmed when you first see this word, let me say at once that you are perfectly right to be. It is in fact the German word for abortion.

But German is a language of unparalleled ambiguity, and so ("those Junkers will cheat you yet!") it also means a place that is out of the way, a retreat or privy.

Never mind the word for 'W.C.' —
what's the Italian for
'Where can I buy some
knickers'?

MONOGRAPH

Once you start on the etymology of euphemisms you
find they are usually based on even older euphemisms.
The word "loo", for instance, which is now common
usage, is an abbreviation of "Waterloo", used in the
nineteenth century as an obvious euphemism for
water-closet.

P.S. There is a village in France called St. Maclou.
Obviously a Scottish saint. The patron saint of sanitary
engineers couldn't possibly have been French.

How to say it when you want it in	
France	Doobler-veh-seh
Italy	Doppio-vee-chee
Germany	Veh-tseh
Spain	Dob-leh-veh-theh
Russia	Vahtair-closét (ВАТЕР-КЛОСЕТ)
Holland	Lavatory or W.C. The Dutch all speak English

Food

FINDING A RESTAURANT
In the best eating countries abroad – that is, in France, Italy and Belgium – the best restaurants are always the most crowded. These are the restaurants to go for.

It is always wise, too, in choosing overnight hotels in the bigger towns to go for those shown in the Michelin *Guide* with the number of rooms in bold type. This is a signal that they have agreed not to be too huffy if you would prefer to go out to dinner, instead of having it in the hotel. If the hotel has a star in Michelin, then eat there, of course; if it hasn't a star, look at the menu displayed outside before you decide.

For all free-lance eating – by which I mean restaurants either *en route*, or which you are free to go to without breach of any *en pension* contract – it is imperative to study the menu before eating.

Avoid restaurants whose outdoor menu includes helpful English translations. The English menu translations *indoors*, on the other hand, don't necessarily signify. One of the best restaurants in the region of Bresse used to translate its excellent *quenelles de brochet à la Nantua* as "pike's balls at the Nantua".

TESTING A RESTAURANT
In France the restaurant with a single Michelin star is the one to aim for. Having earned its medal, it wants to keep it, and so is extra careful about its standards.

The award and non-award of stars by Michelin in its *Guide* to Italy, on the other hand, is pretty confusing in my experience. What possible comparison can there be between the historic and elegant Cambio in Turin, capital of a province that is rich and fertile, full of good meat and wine, and the modest little family hotel Carola

Splendid at Agropoli, south of Salerno, in a region where the meat is very poor, and the fish monotonously Mediterranean? And yet the Cambio and the Carola are both given a star in Michelin, which makes nonsense of the whole system.

I'm afraid I can't tell you if the plat du jour is any good because I always eat next door

BECOMING A REGULAR

Enter any restaurant abroad and you can usually tell at once whether you are going to like it or not. A good restaurant reveals its quality by its atmosphere; décor has nothing to do with food in the eating countries, where they follow the old Yorkshire maxim: "Damn t'décor. Bring on t'bloody dinner!" The quality of a good restaurant will also be reflected in the pleasant facial expressions of its waiters and waitresses. (If you are anti-feminist, forget your prejudices when abroad, or you may starve. Some of the best food in the world is served by waitresses.)

If you decide you like a restaurant on first acquaintance do pay it the compliment of not choosing the cheapest menu. Leave that until next time, for on your second visit you will no longer be a tourist; you will be a *vieux client* and they will be glad to see you and make allowances for any temporary loss of appetite or income from the gaming tables.

I'd complain about the service if I could find a waiter to complain to

ESCAPE ROUTE

As regards eating in Germany and Austria I do not know what advice to give on how to survive – except to leave for Switzerland, Belgium or France as soon as possible.

I know of nothing that makes more depressing reading than the menus displayed outside German or Austrian restaurants. The contents, the repertoire, are identical in every menu. Only the printing or typewriting, the running order of the items, and the prices differ from one menu to another.

FOR "A" LEVEL EATING

In this age, when everybody is mad about education, I must naturally suggest material for further study. Unhesitatingly I recommend two books published by Methuens. They are called *Eating French* and *Eating Italian*, and explain what the traditional, everyday French and Italian dishes should contain if they are to conform honestly to the trades description laws.

You can make yourself a perfect bloody nuisance with these two books in England, too, whenever some upstart caterer tries to sell you warmed-up slices of broiler as *suprême de volaille*, or meatless boiled bones as *osso buco*.

BBC reporters, with their flair for gracious speaking, describe these caterers as "Rester-on-Terze".

En route

GETTING YOUR PRIORITIES RIGHT

As you drive off the boat on to the Continent there are notices to remind you to keep to the right. What no notices tell you is that whatever you may read to the contrary you should always give way to traffic on the right.

I know there are special signs to reassure you that it is your right of way, but until the driver of anything coming into your main road has actually waved you on, it is suicide not to stay where you are. As for anything likely to cross your bows from left to right at a crossing – particularly *your* priority crossing – do not move until it is certain it is giving way to you – that is, stationary, with two flat tyres and a stalled engine.

Every year as we leave England the quaysides are strewn with unaccompanied repatriated cars, whose off-sides are smashed in because their drivers forgot to give *priorité à droite*, and whose near-sides are smashed in because French drivers were damned if they would give any Englishman *priorité à droite*.

ROAD PIGS

If anything ever justified the student barricades of the Events of May 1968, it was the French police. The French police force is manned mainly by Corsicans, on the principle that you set a bandit to catch a bandit. They look brutal and bad-tempered, and they are.

We broke down once on the long, lonely and almost empty road N.154 between Orléans and Chartres. We were completely immobilized. Within a very short time we were relieved to see a police car draw up; at least they'd be able to tell us where there was a garage, and how we could get help. Perhaps even help us improvise something.

Like hell they would. We were gruffly ordered to get our car off the road on to a high grass verge. We managed to push it, my wife and I, while the police stood by and watched.

We asked the policemen if there was a garage anywhere. Yes; three miles along the road in the direction we were facing. As they were driving in that direction themselves would the police be so kind as to ask the garage to send somebody out? No, they wouldn't. And with that they turned round and drove back in the direction they'd come from.

Help eventually came from (but naturally) a passing G.B. car.

Am I being unreasonably xenophobic about those French bastards? Not while I know how any English policeman would help a foreigner in comparable circumstances. And it isn't only the French; the Spanish, and sometimes the Italians, can run them pretty close. "*Vivent les étudiants* of all nations!" I say.

DISC JOCKEYING FOR POSITION

The parking disc, obtainable from the *Mairie* in French towns and petrol stations in Italy, is a guarantee that you can avoid some of the police some of the time. The permitted hours shown on the disc apply to any "blue" parking zone (*disque obligatoire*) in any town in France. The same system applies in Italy – except in Florence, where, our *disco obligatorio* showing 1330-1500 hours, we were pinched parking under a sign which unexpectedly said 1330-1430.

PICNICS

There isn't much the English don't know now about picnicking on the road. Since the war, experience abroad has taught them not only to sit up on chairs at a table like civilized eaters, instead of sitting on rugs and making tea, but that the picnic can be good peptic sense. The vast midday meal consumed by the French and Italians is not for the English to continue road journeys on.

For the English who take their hols in tents, caravans, villas or flats which involve fix-it-yourself eating, the picnic is as essential indoors as out. Apart from anything else it provides an opportunity for choice offered by few restaurants and pensions anywhere. This is particularly so with simple things the hotels, but not the shops, consider are out of season, too classy, or not classy enough – things like figs and artichokes, wild strawberries and a little variety in pâtés and terrines.

NO CASH, BUT NO CARRY

If, like us, you sometimes can't be bothered to cash in the empty wine bottles you have paid a deposit on, do not hesitate to leave them in a prominent position on any French roadside. This is not vandalism; it is the surest way of keeping the countryside tidy. No passing

French peasant can resist taking an empty bottle with a deposit on it.

Plumbing the depths

The English have always made jokes about it, but if there is one thing that has been no laughing matter in France ever since the Romans dejectedly left the country on failing to teach the Gauls the domestic uses of water, it is the plumbing.

A nation which can build the Caravelle and the Citroën has not yet discovered how to instal a yard of the simplest water-piping without an air-lock in it. Sometimes the French can control an air-lock, but they have never learnt to cure one. And even control – a very temporary business at the best of times – usually means only the substitution of one din for another, of a sustained, piercing whine for a shuddering thump.

A hotel restaurant full of commercial travellers in France is a sure sign that the food is good. It is also a guarantee of a disturbed night's rest. The typical air-lock, common to most hotels, is more noticeable where the *voyageurs* spend the night. One such hotel we stayed in was equipped with an air-lock of quite terrifying power and frequency. The slightest turn of a tap anywhere in the building and the whole place rocked to the sound of a quick-firing anti-aircraft gun. The barrage continued until late into the night as one commercial traveller after another brushed his teeth.

It started up again at 5 a.m. when the commercials began to get up and set off on their day's work. There was a lull in the plumbing between 6 and 8 a.m. which

This place is haunted by the ghost of a mad plumber

CLANK! CLANK!

GURGLE! GURGLE!

was filled by a thunderstorm that was most soothing, until it became inaudible when we had to turn on the tap in our own room.

There is only one way to survive the air-lock, and that is to get really sloshed and go to bed before the bombardment.

In Italy it is not the air-lock so much as the water itself that needs keeping under control. In a brand new hotel in Perugia we pushed the handle of a shiny low-level lavatory cistern and the whole thing came away from the wall, with spectacular results.

The trouble about Italy is that they don't yet seem to have discovered Rawlplugs. Electrical and bathroom fittings are fixed into the plaster, and it is only a matter of days before the fittings unfix themselves. Approach all wash basins, cisterns and bedside lamps as gently as possible.

THE ENEMIES OF REPOSE

It is no use thinking that the absence of commercial travellers from a French hotel will necessarily mean fewer disturbances. It may; but when the season of *la chasse* opens in September what, borrowing a phrase from an ancient Baedeker, one may call "the enemies of repose" become a hazard to the English traveller, whether he lie in bed or venture out.

Baedeker was in fact talking about fleas and bed-bugs, but he might just as well have been talking about those intrepid hunters of rabbits, and stalkers of skylarks, who rise at 5 a.m., and brighten the early morning with chatter that can be heard over the drumming of the plumbing.

Extra care should be taken everywhere out of doors at this time of the year. The *chasseurs* in full cry wound, maim and shoot stone dead more fellow-sportsmen and innocent passers-by than they do game. Indeed, the number of human casualties of *la chasse* is exceeded only by that of the French mushroom pickers who poison themselves during the same autumn months.

Two rules, therefore: keep away from all French shooting parties, and never – in *any* country abroad – buy mushrooms at the roadside.

How to survive culture abroad

Like fresh fruit and the chestnut purée and whipped cream of a Mont-Blanc, culture abroad is always better taken in small amounts. This is particularly so with picture galleries.

If you have any feeling for travel at all you can tell at once whether your first visit to a new city or a new country is going to be your last. Nobody, surely, ever believes they will never return to Florence or Venice, Paris or Rome, Naples or Vienna.

Which means that there is no need to try and see every picture in the Uffizi, even during a lengthy stay in Florence. Looking at pictures is the most exhausting, punishing form of culture there is. Even during a five-hour opera you can sleep while culture envelops you, but a picture gallery is sheer footslogging.

On any first visit it is essential to look at the most familiar, most hackneyed pictures in the gallery. The better you know them from reproductions the more overwhelming the first impact of the original will be. If you go to the Louvre in Paris, look at the Mona Lisa, the Venus de Milo, a few Watteaus and that picture of the seductive girl with a bare bottom by Boucher (which ought to be in the Louvre's Salle Rude, but isn't). Leave the rest for next time.

In Florence go to the Uffizi and see the Botticelli room (Room V). It contains the 'Birth of Venus', and the Primavera, which you can enjoy in the company of three of his most beautiful Madonnas, the 'Adoration of the Magi', and an Annunciation. This room is enough of an experience to last until next year.

Florence, in any case, offers wonderful opportunities

for culture while you walk. When you get footsore in the San Lorenzo market you can just drop into the Medici Chapel and relax, looking at the statues by the man John Evelyn always described as "the famous M. Angelo". You then return to your shopping.

A GOOD GUIDE TO PICTURES
The starting point of the trolley bus from Florence to Fiesole is at San Marco, another oasis to enjoy while you wait. The convent is filled with frescoes by Fra Angelico. Look at some of them, take the trolley up to Fiesole, have lunch, and see the rest when you get back.

The door of the church of San Marco displays an unexpected but very reliable guide to pictures in Florence – to the motion pictures, that is, currently showing in the city's fifty-odd cinemas. The guide is published by the ecclesiastical authorities and lists the films in three classes: permitted, adults only, and strictly forbidden to all. The theatres in the third category could not wish for better advertisement, and as a result do a roaring trade.

VENICE OBSERVED
Venice can be a physically very wearying city. As a first-time visitor you can learn a great deal about Venetian art, however, if you limit your tour of the Accademia to three of its twenty-two rooms. They are Room V, which contains nothing but Giovanni Bellini; Room IX, which has a couple of Titians, a spectacular Veronese and several Tintorettos; and Room XX, which is filled with Carpaccio's great sequence of the Legend of St Ursula. (The Room numbers may have changed but not the contents. But it's an easy place to find your way around in.)

On your way from one room to another there is a lot of fine Venetian painting that is likely, as they say, to "rub off on you" – more Titians, more Veroneses, Tintorettos and Tiepolos. Some Guardis too; but for Canalettos, wait till you are next in London. They're better there.

IN RUSSIA, ON THE OTHER HAND...

There is one exception to the rule of picking at, instead of feasting off, picture galleries: Russia. When you are in Moscow see every picture there is in the Museum of Modern Art (now renamed the Pushkin Museum); when you are in St Petersburg (now renamed Leningrad), see every picture there is in the Hermitage.

This is to ensure that you make the most of two superb collections before the Russians can put you in jail, or throw you out of the country for good.

(For the record, the Moscow gallery contains fourteen Monets, ten Renoirs, nine Van Goghs, twenty-two Gaugins, twenty-one Cézannes, forty Matisses, thirty-eight Picassos, seventeen Derains, twelve Bonnards, as well as masterpieces by Signac, Sisley, the Douanier Rousseau, Degas, Vuillard, Manet, Vlaminck and Braque. A Frank Brangwyn, I remember, was hung in a very dark corridor, and was, perhaps deliberately, invisible.)

JUKE BOXES

There is a sinister fascination about other nations' juke boxes. Even the Beatles somehow sound exotic abroad.

It takes a little courage at first, as a foreigner, to pay your money and make your choice. You inevitably feel that what you want to play is likely to bore the pants off the rest of the café customers; or worse, appal them by your bad taste.

Until you learn to identify something They put on which you like, and can go and repeat for yourself after a decent interval, it is best to play safe with classics like Edith Piaf in France, and Domenico (or "Mimi") Modugno in Italy.

Or you can put on another Beatles record.

TIPPING TIP-OFF

In cinemas, theatres and opera houses abroad you are often expected to tip whoever shows you to your seat. In Paris the usherettes are the middle-aged daughters of the old crows who knit for their tips in the gentses; at La Scala in Milan, the ushers wear knee breeches, have big silver chains round their necks and look like Lord Mayors.

The practice of theatre tipping is not universal abroad, but it is as well to be prepared for it, particularly in France and Italy. You can tell whether it is expected, by watching what other people do about it.

ABROAD THROUGH THE TELLY

Foreign television can have the same exotic fascination as the foreign juke box. A great number of hotels seem to have it now; Michelin, however, does not yet show it as though it was an amenity like air-conditioning, as the AA and RAC handbooks do at home.

Mind you, there are still an awful lot of awfully old awful films to put up with wherever you watch the telly abroad. Not only are they so awful that even the BBC hasn't shown them, but they're dubbed, which makes them even less comprehensible. But the commercials are quaint, and if you're feeling really homesick during your next twenty-five annual visits abroad, you can be certain that "La Dynastie des Forsyte" will turn up in the lounge one night.

Perhaps in the foreign version, Soames will turn out to be a drug pusher

La Dynastie des Forsyte

Tricknowledgy

GOOD LANGUAGE

As the Red Queen told Alice (she was talking through her looking glass): "Speak in English when you can't think of the French for a thing."

The trouble about this is that the English words the French understand and use as everyday currency tend to be rather ambiguous. Take the word "shimmy", for instance. What does it mean to you? A dance, perhaps? "I wish I Could Shimmy Like My Sister Kate"? To the French (and the Italians) the word is in common usage as the technical term for wheel-wobble on a car. I learnt this only after I had tried to explain that our car was suffering from "une vacillation des roues antérieures" and was told "Ah! Vous avez le shimmy!"

The development of *le franglais* adds to this sort of ambiguity almost daily. "Un building" means a "tower" of flats or offices. A football seen in a Dieppe sports-shop was called "Le Pass-Over". Even the old-established phrases can be ambiguous. Like "un keep-sake", which is an album of engravings and lithographs given as a present at Christmas or the New Year.

Fashion is probably best served by *franglais*. It provides an easily understood vocabulary – "le pull," "le short", le kilt", "le sweater", and (a direct quote) "la chemise de satin patchwork qui fera un boom dans les boutiques de Paris."

BAD LANGUAGE

A little Italian can be very dangerous, as the actress said to the bishop.

The most common danger is to confuse *fico*, which means a fig, and *fica* which doesn't. With its statutory four letters, *fica*, the dictionary says, is "(vulg) female genitals". Next time you say you don't care a fig for anything, or make your two-fingered gesture of defiance known to Shakespeare as "the fig of Spain" (origin of "fig leaf" perhaps?), you can enjoy the thought that what is quite respectable in England has an extremely rude origin in Italy.

In France be extra careful. It's that ambiguity again. Of course the French for "introduce myself" must be "m'introduire". So what could be easier than for a young Englishman to approach a pretty French girl with "Puis-je m'introduire?"

The girl's reaction to these words is likely to vary from speechless embarrassment to ecstatic anticipation. It depends what kind of girl she is.

The term you should use is "me présenter".

If you are an English girl, you may know that "baiser" means "kiss". So it does. But used as a verb it usually has quite a different connotation in France. If in the course of some friendly diversion or other you happen to say to a Frenchman "baisez-moi" the result may be startling, or welcome, according to how you feel.

"Baiser" is a six-letter word and its use can land you in bed in a matter of moments.

The term you want is "embrassez-moi". Or do you?

DO NOT SPEAK WHEN SPOKEN TO

However little you know of a foreign language, there is a fatal temptation to argue with officials, particularly when you know you are in the wrong.

Once on a train journey from Catania to Turin the ticket inspector said our tickets were not in order. They should have been stamped at the booking office at Genoa, where we had broken our journey; or something. There was a lengthy argument. How was I to know about the booking office? The Minister of Tourism and Spectacles (*Turismo e spettacoli*) himself had given us the tickets, and hadn't said a word about the Genoa booking office.

Our dramatic duet lasted nearly twenty minutes. Eventually the inspector gave up, but warned us not to do it again.

As the inspector left the four Italians in our compartment at once turned to me and asked why on earth I had let on I knew any Italian. Didn't I know that silence was golden, that "aphonia" (Latins love Greek words) was a foreigner's strongest card? My wife agreed with every word they said.

And so, I'm sure, would you.

ONLY A PASSING PHRASE

We are inclined to be rather haughty about those old Phrase Books which told us how to say that our postillion had been struck by lightning, and – surely the most superfluous phrase of all – "You are seasick". But this is an unfair attitude to take. Modern Phrase Books are still compiled on the traditional lines of irrelevance and fantasy.

They don't seem to have the french for - 'could I have a bit more meat with my garlic?'

Phrase Book

Thousands of English travellers set out to survive abroad every year with a phrase book which contains the following bright and useful passage of dialogue:

"My friend thought of buying a motor car."

"We had better send for the doctor."

Another conversation book, used by many motorists anxious for helpful hints in line with contemporary thought, includes a section on visiting the doctor. What the doctor is likely to say to you in French, Italian, Dutch, German, Spanish, Swedish or Danish is marked with an asterisk to denote "medical phrase".

If a Dutch doctor says to you (with asterisk): "Kleedt U uit, gaat U liggen" it means (with asterisk) "Undress, lie down." The Swedish for "Undress, lie down", however, has no asterisk. It is not what the doctor says to you, but what you say to the doctor. Seen any good Swedish films lately?

That the English can survive with my modern Spanish conversation book, just shows that the old bulldog spirit is not dead yet.

You sit in a train and ask the Spaniard next to you: "What station was that?" He replies: "Nuremberg". Unless you both happen to be travelling from **Prague to** Stuttgart this is a damn silly answer to get. As **you are** obviously travelling to Spain (otherwise you wouldn't have a Spanish conversation book, would you?) the most important phrase you need is not included – namely, the Spanish for "Let me out of here!" It is not even in the section headed "Idiotismos".

Nevertheless, there are useful and unusual sequences of dialogue, or rather, monologue. How often has one not been served a meal that merited the comment: "This wine is corked. This meat is not fresh. The vegetables are not cooked. I want tea with bread and butter."

On reflection, one doesn't have to go to Spain to say that. It can be said in English nearly all over England.

However, Spain still has its secrets. Somewhere there is a hotel where, the phrase book tells us, we shall want to know how to ask for "a lift to all doors".

That's something like luxury.

Intercourse with italians

This beats roulette any day.

In 1890 this heading to a section of Baedeker's latest guide to Italy meant only one thing to the reader. Today it will also mean only one thing to the reader.

For today's traveller there is little advice one can offer on what is, after all, a matter of personal taste, opportunity, and unpredictable circumstances. For myself, I recall that Italian girls were rather like the Irish girls a Frenchman was once overheard describing to a fellow countryman. They were beautiful, he said, "mais d'une chasteté formidable!"

Be that (where my own experience of Italy is concerned) as it may, every Englishwoman visiting Italy must be prepared to have her bottom pinched while standing in a bus or staring into a shop window. It is a ritual performed by Italian men of all ages on Englishwomen of all ages.

Its object is principally to make the victim scream. If she doesn't scream (and she should school herself not to) she wins the game, and her opponent will retire, disgraced and humiliated.

As a preliminary to closer relationship bottom-pinching has little significance. Most Italian bottom-pinchers are married, or live with *mamma*, and have no bed to offer anyway. They expect the woman to provide the place and opportunity. Their Fiat 500s, they find, are a little cramped.

Young Englishmen must also expect to have their bottoms pinched by Italian men of all ages – especially in Florence and Venice. No Englishman is safe alone at night in either of those cities.

ETIQUETTE

In Baedeker's obsolete sense of the term, intercourse with foreigners involves the English visitor abroad in other forms of ritualistic behaviour, the most exhausting and inescapable of which is the incessant shaking of hands. I used to think the Germans and Austrians were the worst for this, but they are miles behind the French.

If the habit spread to England, whenever you went into your local you would shake hands with everybody you knew in the bar, including the landlord and the barmaid, and then shake hands with them all again when you left. In England, a nod is still as good as a wink across a crowded room, but it doesn't do abroad, where they get very offended by such things.

CALLING

The hazards of the social call abroad vary very much according to generation and social class. In France the prosperous young – *les jeunes cadres* – will offer you whisky, where their parents will offer you port and sweet biscuits. Austrians and Germans will give you coffee and sticky cakes.

Working-class Italians will bring out a bottle of some very sweet liqueur and insist on you drinking a toast with them at the most inappropiate time of day – half-past ten in the morning, or four in the afternoon.

The less sophisticated Italian will toast you with "chin-chin". He expects all the English to say that and your echo of his toast mustn't disappoint him. After all, he reckons, he is putting you at his ease.

In Italian it is spelt "cin-cin", a happy chance which Cinzano advertising has tumbled to only recently.

TOUJOURS LA POLITESSE

One essential politeness in all countries is to say good-day and goodbye in shops. Gentlemen should also always remove their hats in banks.

The French believe in Liberty, Fraternity and Equality. They do not have a Race Relations Act, for their whites are not the colour problem ours are; but their distinctions between *l'U* and *le non-U* are very marked indeed. On saying goodbye to your hostess you do not say "Au revoir, Madame Dupont" where you would say "Goodbye, Mrs Smith" at home. You say "Au revoir, Madame". The equivalent also applies to Italy and Spain.

Similarly – because it is so easy to pick up the habit, thinking it is a general French custom – you must never greet a married couple with the "Bonjour 'sieur-dame" you hear in cafés. The phrase is about as elegant as saying "Eenin wunner-naw!"

In hotels and pensions abroad those fellow-guests whom you have seen more than once on your way to your regular table at meal times, *must* be greeted, unless you want to be taken for a barbarian. Good-day or good-evening, on entering and leaving is all you need say to show that at least some of us are Europeans.

At restaurants in German-speaking countries a muttered "Mahlzeit" will have to be exchanged with any stranger whose table you're put at, or with any neighbour whose nearby table you aren't.

The phrase means literally "Mealtime", which is all that remains of the ancient rigmarole "I wish you a blessed repast". (The dictionary notes, a little unnecessarily, that "there is no English equivalent".)

Ethnological note: In sailors' brothels in Hamburg it is customary for the satisfied client on his way down the stairs to greet the expectant customer on his way up, with "Mahlzeit".

Conclusions not to be jumped to:

IN FRANCE

That there is any erotic significance in the words Sex Rouge, Sex Noir and Sex Percia printed on the large-scale (1:200.000) Michelin map No 70. They are mountains respectively 9535 ft, 9044 ft, and 8217 ft high. I trust this information will save you a fruitless journey.

That Muscadet is a sweet wine. It is dry and white and has nothing to do with muscatel.

That when you read how twenty schoolchildren suffered "intoxication" they were drunk. They were overcome by poisonous fumes.

That the advertisements all over France for "Piles

Wonder" advertise anything except electric torch batteries.

That if you are a girl and feeling hot you should say to a young man "Je suis chaude". Say "J'ai chaud". The famous pianist Harriet Cohen once exclaimed "Je suis chaude" to a group of modern composers at a contemporary music festival. I was there. The expression of horror, apprehension and downright disbelief on the faces of the composers was worth every penny of the fare to Salzburg to see.

IN ITALY

That if you ask for a casino they'll take you to a casino. They will take you to a brothel. What *you* call a "casi'no" they call a "casino'."

That, because you are musical, "Allegro" means fast. It means cheerful, gay, good-humoured. It also means sloshed.

That, because you are musical, "Largo" means slow. It means broad, and in Palermo and Venice a square is a Largo.

That the road sign "Adagio" has anything to do with dancers. It means drive slowly.

That when a picture is described as "suggestivo" it means anything more than romantically picturesque.

That "mostarda" is what you need when you want mustard. *Mostarda* is a sweet-sour pickle. What you want is "senape".

That *zuppa inglese* is either a soup or English. In case you hoped it might be Brown Windsor, it is the Italian for trifle.

IN GERMANY

That "Schellfisch" means what it looks like. It means haddock.

*How to survive
the english abroad*

"As an English man does not travel to see English men,
I retired to my room."

Sterne: *A Sentimental Journey*

*How the english
can survive your return*

Everybody hopes for a sympathetic audience for their
travellers' tales. Colour transparencies tell only half the
story; the ones I take are so bad they tell no story at all.

Holiday snaps, travellers' tales or not, there is one rule
to be ruthlessly observed: avoid using the original
names for foreign towns when there are familiar
English equivalents. To do so is not only a madly
irritating affectation, but it is not very good manners.
Some of your audience may never have been abroad
and so will not understand you if you say "Wien" for
Vienna, "München" for Munich, "Firenze" for
Florence, "Livorno" for Leghorn, "Praha" for Prague,
"Marseille" for Marseilles, "Napoli" for Naples,
"Boulogne" for Boulogne, "Torino" for Turin,
"Mantova" for Mantua, or "Padova" for Padua.

On the other hand, I think it is imperative to pronounce
"Lyon" in the French way and not call it "Lyons".
This is entirely to avoid misunderstanding. If you say
you lunched at Lyons and had *quenelles de brochet au
gratin, volaille demi-deuil, fonds d'artichauts au foie
gras,* and a bottle of Moulin-à-Vent, you will give an
entirely false impression.

You did not lunch at "Lyons" but at "Lyon". And at
la Mère Brazier's, what's more.

Truths spring eternal

'The presence of ladies generally adds considerably to
the expenses of the party.'

Baedeker 1894

'Only dogs and foreigners walk in the sun. Christians
walk in the shade.'

Roman Proverb (from Baedeker 1913)

'The affix Esq. should be omitted from all letters sent
poste restante.'

Baedeker 1898

[*Author's note :* If it is not omitted, your letter will be
pigeon-holed under "E". This really happened to me
not long ago.]

'In the case of riot or other popular disturbance, the
stranger should get out of the way as quickly as possible,
as the careful policemen, in order to prevent the escape
of the guilty, are apt to arrest anyone they can lay
hands on.'

Baedeker 1898

'The native waiter often pays more attention to his
dignity as Caballero than to the artistic performance of
his duties.'

Baedeker, *Spain* (1913)

'. . . on the Alps
'It is reported thou didst eat strange flesh
'Which some did die to look on.'

Shakespeare, *Antony and Cleopatra*

'Plus ça change, plus c'est la même chose.'

Alphonse Karr

[*Historical note:* Alphonse Karr, b. Paris 1808, d. St Raphaël, 1890. He discovered St Raphaël when it was a fishing village, settled there, encouraged its development, and by the time he died it was known as the Bournemouth of the Riviera. He was – as you may have guessed – a satirical and humorous writer.]

IN EXTREMIS	
The Pawnshop	
France:	*le Mont de piété*
Italy:	*il Monte di pietà*
Spain:	*el Monte de piedad*
Germany:	*das Leihaus*
Russia:	the *Lombard*